Glendurgan Garden
CORNWALL

G000068734

A souvenir guide

 THE NATIONAL TRUST

A GARDEN FOR ALL AGES

Glendurgan has developed continuously over the last 180 years. It is renowned for its trees and shrubs, which provide foliage and flowers for an ever-changing view of colours and textures. The garden nestles in a lush valley and you can glimpse the beautiful Helford River throughout. It has always been a family garden, and the Maze and Giant's Stride continue to provide amusement for all ages.

A piece of heaven on Earth

Glendurgan is a secret and special garden. It lies hidden from the outside world by shelter belts of woodland, below which are three of Cornwall's narrow and beautiful coastal valleys. But Glendurgan also looks outwards, with views down to the fishing village of Durgan and the broad estuary of the Helford River. The garden was created from the 1820s by Alfred Fox, who came from a prosperous family of Falmouth ship agents, and used his foreign contacts to collect exotic new plants from all over the world. They have flourished here thanks to Glendurgan's moist, almost sub-tropical climate.

Fox was a devout Quaker, and his religious beliefs are reflected in the trees planted on the Holy Bank. Glendurgan was to be a piece of heaven on Earth, and so it remains.

A perennial delight

Glendurgan is at its most colourful in the spring, when the mounds of hybrid camellias and rhododendrons complement the delicate primroses, violets and wild daffodils that speckle the steep, grassy banks. The summer brings myrtles, hydrangea and eucryphia. Then later in the year the contrasting textures and shapes of bamboos, conifers, and palms come into their own.

Opposite The giant tulip tree in the Cherry Orchard was planted by Alfred Fox

Far left A view of Helford River from the house in the 1860s; a watercolour by Rachel Elizabeth Fox

Left The same view today

TOUR OF THE GARDEN

1 THE CAMELLIA WALK

Approached from a curved path laid out in 1993, this is planted with modern *Camellia reticulata* cultivars, such as 'Purple Gown' and 'Noble Pearl', interplanted with summer- and autumn-flowering bulbs and perennials. On the straight path, some of the camellias are over 100 years in age and include 'Inspiration' and japonica 'Nobilissima', both of which were probably planted by George Fox. He was an enthusiastic plantsman who acquired many newly introduced shrubs from his cousin at the nearby garden of Penjerrick. Later plantings of 'Captain Rawes', 'Cornish Snow', 'Debutante' and many other cultivars create colourful pictures in the spring. Notable rhododendrons include R. 'Saffron Queen', 'Lady Alice Fitzwilliam' and groups of azalea (*R. luteum*).

2 THE CHERRY ORCHARD

Alfred Fox planted this area with cherry and pear trees in the mid-1820s, hence its name. On the northern side are two magnificent tulip trees, about 175 years old, and some deciduous azaleas and eucryphias. In the valley are a Pocket Handkerchief (Ghost) Tree, with its strange white bracts in May, magnolias and a selection of flowering cherries, all with predominantly white flowers. On the southern slopes is a group of the lavender-blue *Rhododendron augustinii*, planted with various white-flowered cherries. In the spring these banks are covered with daffodils, followed by primroses, primulas, bluebells and aquilegia.

3 MANDERSON'S HILL

This is clothed with some notable trees, including some rare and tender conifers which can be grown only in the mildest areas of Britain. Chusan Palms (*Trachycarpus fortunei*), the myrtles with their distinctive peeling bark near the lower path, and Winter Bark (*Drimys winteri*) also add to the sub-tropical character of this part of the garden. As you descend to Durgan Village at the far end of the hill, you can see the parallel stone walls of the Cattle Rush, a drive allowing cows to be brought down to the stream to drink.

4 THE LOWER VALLEY

In the moist and sheltered deep valley, bamboos and tree ferns thrive. Many plants from Australia and New Zealand are grown by the Bamboo Bridge, including the Sword Tree or Lancewood. In the lower part of the valley beyond the *Magnolia campbellii* 'Alba' are large groups of various hydrangeas, Portuguese Laurels and rhododendrons.

OPPOSITE

Top The Bamboo Bridge in the Lower Valley

Below left The path in the Cherry Orchard wends through wild spring flowers and rhododendrons

Below right *Rhododendron augustinii* 'Electra' flowering in May

5 DURGAN VILLAGE

The hamlet consists of some 20 cottages, which were originally almost entirely occupied by fishermen – the Helford River and Falmouth Bay are still renowned for pilchards, mackerel, lobster and crabs. The fishermen's catches were taken into Falmouth market by donkeys, which during the summer freely roamed around the fields surrounding the village and in winter lived in cellars in Durgan. Part of one of these cellars now provides an interpretation room showing historic pictures of Durgan and its inhabitants.

Some of the cottages are now available for holiday accommodation, three being owned by the National Trust. They all look across the Helford River towards The Lizard. Further up the river on the other shore lies Frenchman's Creek, made famous by the novelist Daphne du Maurier. There is now a scheduled ferry that provides access to other parts of the Helford during the holiday season.

6 BIRCH'S ORCHARD

The western valley has a colour scheme in which yellow, blue and mauve predominate. The spring-flowering bog arums, king cups and drifts of daffodils are followed by various rhododendrons, hydrangeas and yellow hypericum. At the valley head, above the group of tree ferns and mimosa (*Acacia dealbata*), an old cider press has been placed in this former orchard. From near the recently built School Room (on the site of a building erected for the education of local children) it is possible to spot the Helford River through the trees.

7 THE OLIVE WALK

This relatively new and informal walk connects the pets' grave and Holy Bank area to the School Room. You will miss the Giant's Stride unless you double back later. The olives were planted in the early 1990s amid an area of trees which served as a wind break. The warm south-facing area is perfect for the eleven varieties of olive grown here. The area has also been planted with other Mediterranean crop-producing plants such as figs and pecan nuts. There were olive trees at Glendurgan before the existing plants took root – in the early 20th century, George Fox recorded that the Fox family, who at the time exported pilchards to Italy, received a present of olive trees from an Italian fishing contact.

Below Helford River glimpsed from Birch's Orchard

Opposite Durgan village

Left Three of the cottages in Durgan are available as National Trust holiday accommodation

8 THE GIANT'S STRIDE

From the top of a stout pole hang six strong ropes, from which generations of Fox family children have swung: try it yourself. Take care and always choose a handle higher than your head. When most of the ropes are taken, race around the pole. You will soon become airborne – hence the name, 'The Giant's Stride'.

9 THE SCHOOL ROOM WALK

This path, dominated by woodland trees, led to the old school in Birch's Orchard. Nearer the house are a Californian Redwood (*Sequoia sempervirens*), a fine *Magnolia* x *veitchii* 'Peter Veitch', some Irish Yews and a medlar. You can also find a touching memorial to the family's dogs.

10 THE MAZE AND THE POND

The maze was planted by Alfred Fox in 1833, using Cherry Laurel (*Prunus laurocerasus*). His inspiration was the then famous maze in the Sydney Gardens, Bath. The thatched summer-house follows the design of the original, and four Chusan Palms punctuate the hedges.

On the island in the centre of the nearby pond is a Deodar Cedar, while to the north there is a large weeping Swamp Cypress. Below the pond are two rare Chinese firs, *Cunninghamia lanceolata* and *C. lanceolata* 'Glauca'.

11 THE HOLY BANK

Gathered here are the Tree of Heaven, the Judas Tree, the Crown of Thorns and, nearby, a recently planted Glastonbury Thorn (*Crataegus monogyna* 'Biflora').

Right Giant *Agave americana* flowering in 2004

12 THE VALLEY HEAD

Beneath the house is a small goldfish pond, surrounded by ferns, banana trees and other exotic plants. The path allows fine views to be enjoyed down the valley towards the Helford River. Here is a wide variety of trees and shrubs, including cistus, tea trees, grevilleas, a group of Puya, a Chinese Persimmon, a blue-grey Arizona Cypress and a *Rhododendron yakushimanum* with its felt-covered new leaves in spring. Beyond a wonderful *Cornus kousa*, the spiky leaves of an *Agave americana* dominate the view back to the house. This is the remaining replacement plant from a group that spectacularly flowered during the summer of 2004. The taller of the two flower spikes reached over eight metres and contributed to the striking, sub-tropical atmosphere of this special Cornish garden. If you look back to the Holy Bank, you will see that the valley is planted with a selection of *Penjerrick rhododendrons*.

Amazing facts

- Alfred Fox had a total of twelve children and so the maze may well have been created to entertain them! The maze was also popular with adults – in 1854, Elizabeth Tuckett wrote in her diary, 'We dined in the house and then lay in the grass and sang until we joined the gentlemen who had retired to the labyrinth to smoke.'

- The hedges are kept at a height of three to four feet (up to 120cm) partly for ease of maintenance and partly to make it less daunting to children.

- Maintaining the maze is relatively straightforward: we cut it four to five times a year and feed the hedges once a year. It takes three people a day to cut it and a day to remove the clippings.

- Up to 75,000 people walk (or run!) through the maze each year.

Above The maze was planted in 1833 and is enjoyed to this day

GLENDURGAN AND THE FOX FAMILY

The Fox family has lived in the Falmouth area since the mid-18th century. With the development of Falmouth as a fishing port, mail depot and deep-water anchorage for transatlantic shipping, the Foxes moved their business here in 1762. The Foxes had the means to buy country estates all along the nearby coast, where they could satisfy their shared loved of gardening – at Goonvrea, Penjerrick, Tredrea, Trebah and at Glendurgan.

THE CREATION OF GLENDURGAN

Below Fox sculpture at the visitor entrance to the garden. It is a re-creation of the original garden gates, now at the private entrance to the Fox family home

1820

Alfred Fox rented fish cellars and orchards in Durgan from this date. The Fox family lived and worked in Falmouth, and fishing was one of their business interests. Alfred was attracted to Durgan because of the fish and shellfish that were landed there, and the orchards that benefited from the sheltered climate in the valley behind the village.

The family were Quakers and keen gardeners, trying to create a small piece of heaven on earth in the various gardens they established in and around Falmouth. The Holy Bank is one of the more pronouncedly instructive features. In the early 19th century, the family firm prospered from Cornwall's Industrial Revolution and the Falmouth Packet Mail Service.

1826

Alfred had a thatched cottage built at the top of the main valley above Durgan. He and his wife Sarah started work on clearing the three valleys, extended and planted orchards, and created a trout pond. For shelter they added all kinds of trees, including lime, beech, sycamore, oak and ash, as well as various evergreens, including Holm Oaks, and conifers newly introduced from North America.

1829

Despite having a family of twelve, and perhaps due to that, Sarah started and ran the first school in the Mawnan Smith area, which was in the Pound House. This is on the site of what is now the re-created School Room. The school continued to prosper until 1842.

1837

Whilst having lunch in Falmouth, Alfred was informed that his cottage had burnt to the ground. He burst out laughing, delighted that this apparent disaster had solved a problem for him: at the time, he had been discussing the accommodation for his increasing family. A new house was built on a slightly larger scale.

'In terms of concept, inspiration and sentiment, [Glendurgan] is still very much a Fox garden. The family did not have the benefit of horticultural expertise, yet they created a perfectly harmonious garden, which evolved through trial and error, as well as by the application of aesthetic considerations'

Charles Fox, *Glendurgan*

Right An old guide to the maze in Sydney Gardens, Bath, which provided the model for the Glendurgan maze

Below The original thatched cottage built in 1826 with orchards being tended and the Helford River in the distance.

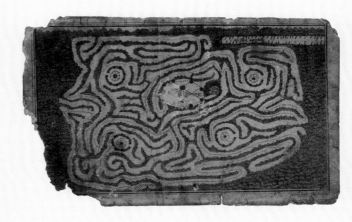

1876

Alfred's son-in-law, Sir Joseph Pease, created a new and more permanent school and reading room on the quay at Durgan, now a National Trust holiday cottage.

1891

Alfred's son George extended the house and took over the garden. The structure of the garden was already well established, and he was content to add ornamental trees and shrubs, as well as continuing the cultivation of fruit trees, which bore apples, pears, nectarines, peaches, figs, greengages and citrus fruits.

1923

George Fox wrote that Glendurgan 'has been so enjoyed and loved by father and mother's descendants that it seems almost a family duty to carry on there as a family home if possible in the hope of future generations being privileged and able to do the same.'

1962

George's son Cuthbert with his wife Moyra and son Philip gave the garden to the National Trust, which was the year in which the family firm, G.C. Fox & Co, reached its bi-centenary. With the sixth generation of the Fox family still living at Glendurgan, their gift has allowed the spirit of conservation and innovation created by Alfred Fox to continue for the enjoyment of all visitors to the garden.

Left This piece of heaven on Earth enjoyed by generations of Foxes, now preserved for the enjoyment of all; from a watercolour by Rachel Elizabeth Fox

Sizeable fruit

The Fox family liked to record their success in growing huge pieces of fruit. In 1831 Alfred noted that he had 'gathered a gooseberry 4.25 inches [10.6cm] in circumference'. In 1897 George wrote, 'Billy brought in citrus, one measured 1'10.5" [56.3cm] round the long way and 1'9" [47.5cm] the short way (the waist). It would just squeeze into my hat endways but would not go in the long way.'

Locally grown produce, most of it from the Helford River area, can be enjoyed in the restaurant and purchased in the shop.

Left Durgan village with the
garden behind it

ASPECTS OF GLENDURGAN

This typical Cornish valley garden enjoys one of the mildest climates in Britain. Because of its sheltered position, it misses most of the strong and cold winds, and because of its proximity to the sea it is usually frost-free.

Gardening at Glendurgan

Frosts are rare at Glendurgan because the cold air 'drains' out to sea, and the mixed woods either side of the valley are vital to protect the garden from strong winds. The soil is lime-free, but not naturally rich. The 25 acres (10ha) of the garden and 15 acres of wind-break woodland are currently maintained by three gardeners and a number of dedicated volunteers, whose work is made more difficult by the steep slopes, where access for machinery is awkward.

Year-round interest

Glendurgan is made up of three well-watered valleys, which are nearly sub-tropical – growing here is a range of plants seldom seen elsewhere in this country. It is known as a springtime garden, but has a great deal of interest in summer and autumn also.

Opposite The view across the valley in the spring looking towards the tulip tree

What makes a Cornish garden?

- Cornwall is rich in minerals, slate and granite, which make the soil acidic.

- The climate is warm and humid, caused by the Gulf Stream and approximately 113cm of rain per year.

- Indigenous hills and valleys underpin Cornish garden landscape.

SEASONAL TREASURES

February	Camellias, snowdrops, primroses
March	Magnolias, daffodils, camellias
April	Rhododendrons, magnolias
May	Bluebells, azaleas, candelabra primulas, embothrium
June	Aquilegia, cornus, Geranium palmatum
July	Myrtles, agapanthus
August	Hydrangeas, eucryphia
September	Amaryllis, cyclamen
October	Autumn colour, nerines
At all times	Gunnera, bamboo, ferns and palms

WILD FLOWER MEADOWS

All of the grass areas within the garden are maintained as spring wild flower areas. These are awash with flowering bulbs early in the year, including snowdrops, daffodils and bluebells. The show of wild flowers continues with primroses, followed by aquilegia, campion and more, including hundreds of wild orchids.

Right View from the Cherry Orchard looking through the old oak tree to the laurel maze

How do we create the wild flower areas?

- In early spring we weed the banks thoroughly to remove unwanted species.
- The areas are then left to flower and set seed. This can be an untidy time but it is essential to allow seed to fill gaps, aid the spread of welcome species and provide new plants.
- From early July we start to cut the grass and flower stems, and leave them to dry for a week or two. This allows the seed to drop and insects to escape. It is then composted and used as mulch.
- By removing the grass before it has a chance to decompose, we are not putting nutrients back into the soil. On top of this, we use only fertilisers and mulch immediately around plants, starving the soil. Poorer soil results in shorter, weaker grass – but large numbers of wild flowers.
- After leaf fall in December all of these areas are cut, and the grass and leaves removed again.
- New species can be introduced by seed or plugs, as long as we ensure they are not invasive – if they are, they will take over from local species.

If you have enjoyed Glendurgan, why not visit the National Trust's gardens at Trelissick, Feock, near Truro, and Trengwainton, Madron, near Penzance?